A boy had a pet fly named Fly Guy.
Fly Guy could say the boy's name —

Buzz and Fly Guy arrived at the dog show. They were there to see different types of dogs compete for a grand prize.

"Look!" Buzz said, pointing to a sign. "These dogs are from all over the world. This one is French."

Oh là là!

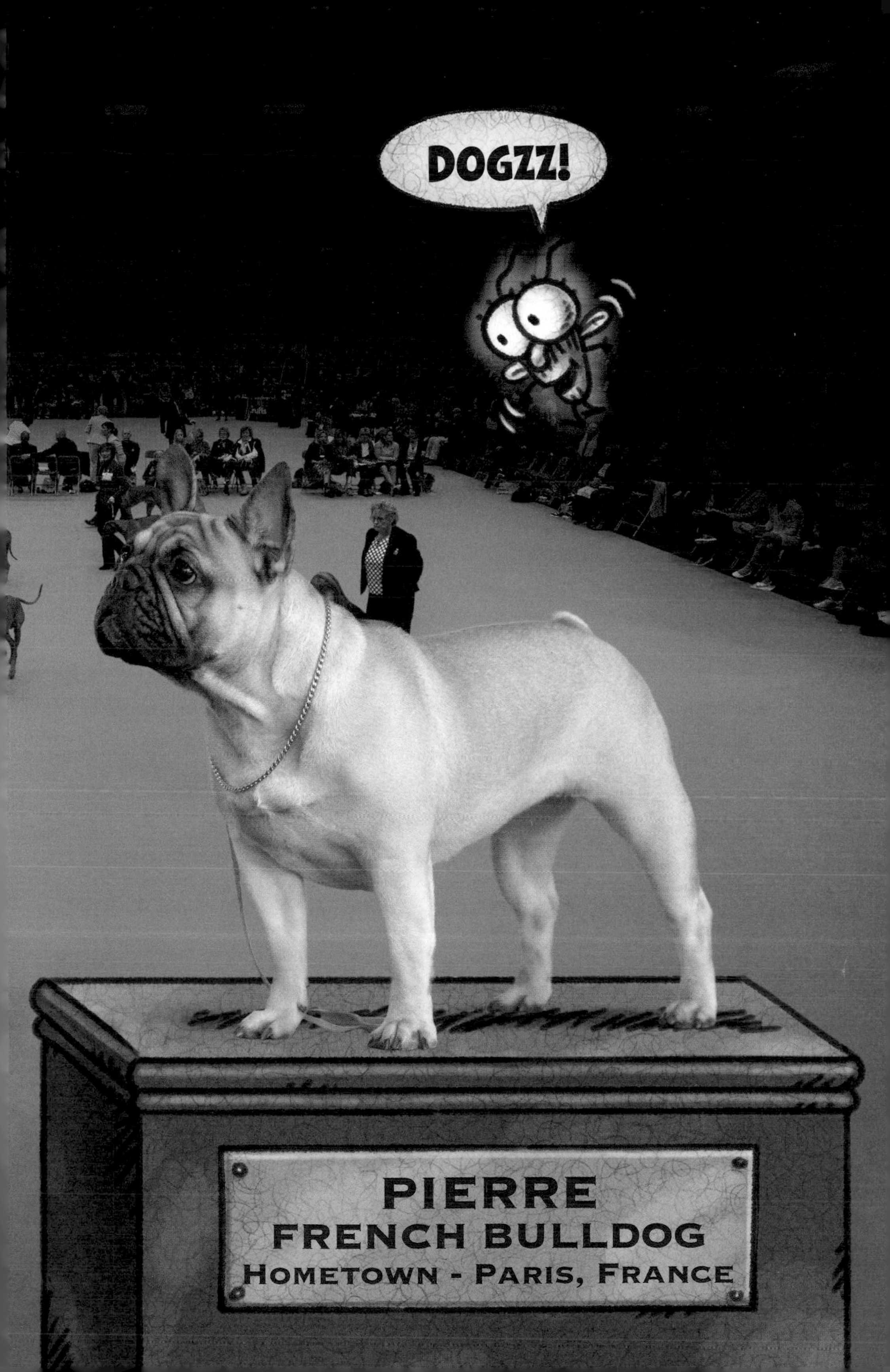
DOGZZ!
PIERRE
FRENCH BULLDOG
HOMETOWN - PARIS, FRANCE

Just like people, dogs come in all different shapes and sizes. The best of each type, or breed, are chosen to be show dogs.

The Scottish terrier has often won the top prize—or "Best in Show"—at dog shows!

The slim saluki (suh-**loo**-kee) is a hunting dog and one of the oldest dog breeds in the world.

Pekingese (pee-ki-**neez**) are a toy breed. That means they are small dogs that are kept as pets. This dog was popular among rulers in ancient China.

Dalmatians are known as "coach dogs." They were bred to guard horses and coaches. These smart, loyal dogs became popular as fire dogs.

What did the Dalmatian say when he scratched an itch?

FLEAZZ?

Ahhh, that's the spot!

Dogs are members of the canine—or canid—family. Foxes, wolves, jackals, and coyotes are also canines. Scientists believe gray wolves and modern dogs are both related to the same extinct wolf species.

POLAR FOX

GRAY WOLF

JACKAL

○ SIBERIAN HUSKY ○

○ GERMAN SHEPHERD ○

Some dogs still look like their wolf cousins, while others don't. The shih tzu is more closely related to wolves than the German shepherd is. You wouldn't know to look at it!

○ SHIH TZU ○

What do wolves love the most?

FLEAZZ?

Howlidays.

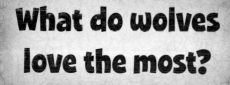

Dogs and wolves have many things in common. They both howl to communicate.

North American gray wolf

Beagle puppy

They both have a strong sense of smell.

Red wolf

Chocolate Labrador

Wolves and dogs are both social animals.

Timber wolves

BOTH HAZZ FLEAZZ?

Still, dogs and wolves are very different. Wolves are wild. Dogs became tame between 15,000 and 40,000 years ago. That means dogs changed over time to live with humans as pets.

Dogs have smaller brains and skulls than similar-sized wolves.

Wolves aren't easily tamed. But dogs can be trained to pull a sled, to play catch in the park, and to perform in dog shows!

The American Kennel Club has a registry, or an official list, of more than 190 recognized dog breeds.

The smallest breeds include the Chihuahua (chi-**wah**-wuh), Japanese Chin, Yorkshire terrier, Pomeranian, affenpinscher (**a**-fuhn-pin-shur), and papillon (pah-pee-**yohn**).

Chihuahuas are a national symbol of Mexico.

Japanese Chin are known for acting like cats!

The popular Yorkie usually weighs less than 7 pounds.

Affenpinschers are known for being fun.

Papillon means "butterfly" in French. It refers to the shape of this dog's frilly ears.

What is it called when a cat wins a dog show?

FLEAZZ!

A cat-has-trophy!

The world's largest dog breeds include the Great Dane, Old English mastiff (**ma**-stif), Newfoundland (**noo**-fuhnd-luhnd), Great Pyrenees (**peer**-uh-neez), and Bernese (bur-**neez**) mountain dog.

When standing on its hind legs, a full-grown Great Dane will be taller than most people!

When the Pilgrims sailed on the *Mayflower* in 1620, they brought two dog breeds with them. They were the spaniel and the Old English mastiff.

Newfoundlands have partially webbed feet! This makes them great swimmers who are skilled at water rescues.

The Great Pyrenees was bred to guard herds while shepherds slept. They often bark at night.

The Bernese mountain dog has an easygoing temper. It loves spending time outdoors.

Why aren't dogs good dancers?

FLEAZZ?

Because they have two left feet!

No matter the breed, dogs have many things in common. Dogs see color differently than humans. Their eyes see only blue and yellow light. Dogs see only in combinations of these two colors.

DOG VISION COLOR SPECTRUM

DOG VISION

HUMAN VISION

Human noses have about 5 million special cells that detect odors. Dog noses have closer to 225 million! That makes a dog's nose 1,000 times more sensitive than a human's nose. And every dog's nose print has its own pattern—just like a human fingerprint!

Dogs spend about half of the day sleeping. They dream just like humans do.

zzzzzZZ

While some dogs have been bred to be pets, others were born to work.

Collies, sheepdogs, and corgis are herd dogs. They protect sheep, cattle, and other livestock on farms and ranches. Other herding dogs, such as the German shepherd, are popular police dogs.

Many dogs work in search and rescue. They might help find a lost hiker. They might locate someone trapped in snow after an avalanche. Golden and Labrador retrievers are often used on these missions.

Why couldn't the dog play tennis?

FLEAZZ?

It was a boxer!

One important job a dog can have is to be a guide for people who are blind or have other disabilities. Labrador retrievers and golden retrievers are great fits for this work. They are smart, loyal, and gentle.

These puppies begin training when they are around 8 weeks old. They learn to stop at curbs and stairs, go around bumps, and obey their owner's commands.

Okay, no more jokes, because you only say "fleas."

PLEAZZ?

Check out these famous dogs!

In 1925, 100 sled dogs saved the children of Nome, Alaska. They relayed medicine to the town from 700 miles away during a crisis. Two dogs—Balto and Togo—became famous for leading the others through a blizzard.

A statue of Balto in New York City's Central Park.

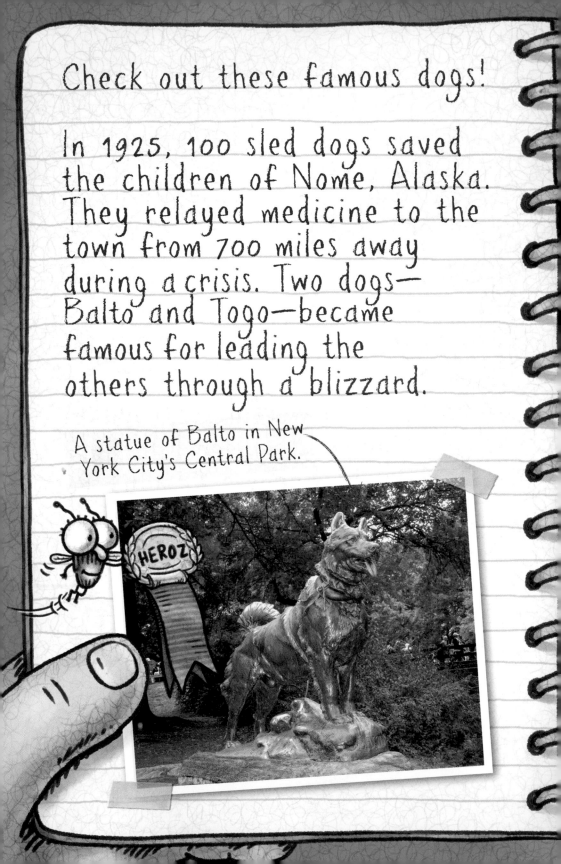

HEROZ

During World War I, a terrier named Stubby served with American soldiers in France. He cheered up wounded soldiers and kept troops safe by sniffing out deadly gas. He even caught a German spy!

In 2017, two powerful earthquakes struck Mexico. A golden Labrador named Frida became famous for saving the lives of 12 people. Frida is named for the painter Frida Kahlo. There is even a mural painted in Mexico City in the dog's honor.

Dog breeds have a lot in common, but they are different, too.

The Catahoula (ka-tuh-**hoo**-luh) leopard dog is a hunting dog. It can climb trees when chasing prey!

Almost all newborn Siberian husky puppies have blue eyes. But around 2 to 8 weeks after birth, the dog's eye color may start to change. By the time a husky is 12 to 16 weeks old, it might have blue eyes, brown eyes, or even one brown and one blue eye!

MORE JOKEZ PLEAZZ.

English bulldogs pass a lot of gas! That's because these pups have trouble eating many foods. Bad foods cause gas to build up in their stomachs. To feel better, they should eat a healthy diet and get plenty of exercise.

Yodel-lay-he-hoo!

The basenji (buh-**sen**-jee) is a small African hound that doesn't bark. Instead, these dogs use a high-pitched howl that's similar to a yodel.

Greyhounds are the fastest dogs around. They can run at a speed of 35 miles per hour for up to seven miles! In fact, greyhounds can run faster than the fastest human. And while a cheetah would win in a short sprint, the greyhound would easily outrun the cheetah in a longer race.

Most dogs have pink tongues, but two dogs are known for their blue-black tongues. They are the chow chow and the Chinese shar-pei (shahr-**pay**).

Dalmatian puppies are born white! Their spots develop as they grow older.

There are two types of the Chinese crested dog. One has fur and one does not. The hairless version has smooth, spotted skin and tufts of hair on its head, tail, and ankles.

The puli (**poo**-lee) has a unique fur coat. The soft, wooly, dense undercoat is covered by long waterproof hair that naturally forms cords.

JOKEZ PLEAZZ!

Dogs Around the World

The first dogs to spend a day in space before returning to Earth were Belka and Strelka. They were launched on the Russian *Sputnik 5* spacecraft in 1960.

Pekingese are one of the oldest dog breeds in the world. They were bred to look like small lions and were worshipped in ancient China.

Queen Elizabeth II of England is known for her love of corgis. She has owned more than 30 since 1933.

Many American presidents have had dogs. Recent White House residents include President Biden's German shepherds, Champ and Major.

Two of the world's most popular dog breeds are the Australian shepherd and the rottweiler (**raht**-wye-lur). The rottweiler was ranked the number-one dog in 34 different countries!

There are more than 75 million pet dogs in the United States—more than in any other country!

Buzz and Fly Guy's Tips for Choosing the Perfect Pet:

- Adopt, don't shop! More than 3 million dogs enter animal shelters every year in the United States. These animals are all looking for new homes.

- Do your research. Read up on different dog breeds to find the right one for your family. If you live in an apartment building in a city, a small dog might be the perfect fit. Have a house in the country? Maybe a large breed is for you!

- Decide whether you want a playful puppy or a more mature dog. Both are great, but they will have different needs.

- Be sure you're ready. Having a pet is a big job! Dogs require food, water, regular walks, exercise, grooming, training, and, most important, lots of love!

"I can't believe how much we learned about dogs today," Buzz said. "I can't wait for our next adventure!"